# I Like Science!

# Visiting VOLCANOES

## with a Scientist

*Catherine McGlone*

**Enslow Publishers, Inc.**

40 Industrial Road          PO Box 38
Box 398                        Aldershot
Berkeley Heights, NJ 07922   Hants GU12 6BP
USA                            UK
http://www.enslow.com

# Contents

# Words to Know

**earthquake (URTH kwayk)—A shaking of the ground. Earthquakes happen when rock moves below the earth's surface.**

**erupt (ee RUPT)—To explode, as when lava shoots out of the hole of a volcano.**

**lava (LAH vuh)—Melted rock coming from a volcano or crack in the earth.**

**magma (MAG muh)—Melted rock inside the earth.**

**mineral (MIHN ur uhl)—A solid natural substance, like a diamond, that comes out of the ground.**

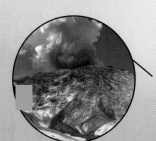

**volcano (vahl KAY noh)—An opening in the earth's surface where lava, pieces of rock, and hot gas come out. Most volcanoes look like mountains.**

Imagine how
surprised people
were the first
time they saw a
volcano erupt.

They must
have had many
questions.

3

She is a volcano scientist. She finds out how volcanoes work. She learns about volcanoes by asking questions.

4

She tells people who live near
volcanoes what might happen
when a volcano erupts.

# What is a volcano?

Hot gas, melted rock, and bits of rock blow out of a hole in the earth. The rock cools and piles up around the hole. This forms a volcano.

Some volcanoes are very small.
Others erupt over and over again
and grow to be large mountains.

magma

The inside of the earth is very hot. To cool off, the earth lets go of the heat. Heat melts the earth's rock. The melted rock is called magma.

When magma comes
out of the volcano, it
is called lava.

# How can scientists tell when a volcano will erupt?

Scientists look for clues.
Often there are earthquakes
under the volcano.

Many times the volcano sends gas out of its hole. Sometimes the volcano gets fatter or thinner.

Mt. St. Helens, 1980, a few weeks before it erupted

# How do scientists find these clues?

They use special tools
that measure the gas.
The tools tell how
much gas is coming
out of the volcano.

A lot of gas is a clue that the
volcano may be ready to erupt.

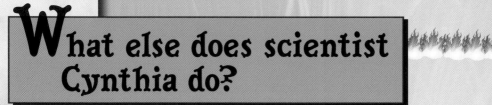

Scientist Cynthia looks at rocks she finds on volcanoes. She breaks the rocks open and looks at them with a hand lens.

14

minerals

There are minerals inside the rock. The
rock was made deep inside the earth.
The minerals show just *how* deep the
rocks were.

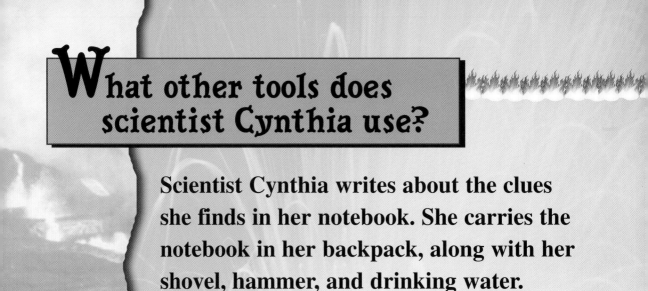

# What other tools does scientist Cynthia use?

Scientist Cynthia writes about the clues she finds in her notebook. She carries the notebook in her backpack, along with her shovel, hammer, and drinking water.

16

She uses the clues she finds to
make maps of the volcano area.

Cynthia made this map. It shows
different areas of lava that came
out of volcanoes in Oregon. Each
color stands for a different age
of lava.

# Where are volcanoes found?

ASIA

NORTH AMERICA

Ring of Fire

Pacific Ocean

Equator

AUSTRALIA

SOUTH AMERICA

•=volcano.

Volcanoes are found around the world.
Most volcanoes are in the Ring of Fire.
Scientist Cynthia has visited volcanoes
in many places.

Sometimes she looks at volcanoes from a helicopter. She loves being outdoors to do her job!

Scientist Cynthia studies mountains in Oregon called the Three Sisters. The ground there gives her clues that it may become a new volcano.

It may be 10 or 100 or 1,000 years before a new volcano forms. Cynthia will keep watching!

# Can you make your own volcano?

**You will need:**

- ✔ empty yogurt cup
- ✔ baking sheet
- ✔ play dough or clay
- ✔ measuring cup
- ✔ water
- ✔ tablespoon
- ✔ baking soda
- ✔ vinegar

1. Place an empty yogurt cup on a baking sheet.

2. Mold play dough or clay into a volcano shape around the yogurt cup. Leave the opening at the top uncovered.

3.  Pour $\frac{1}{4}$ cup of water into the container. Stir in 1 tablespoon of baking soda.

4.  Pour $\frac{1}{4}$ cup of vinegar into the container.

5.  Watch what happens!

What happens if you repeat the experiment and add less vinegar? What happens if you add more vinegar?

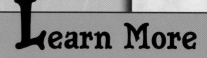

## Books

Berger, Melvin, and Gilda Berger. *Why Do Volcanoes Blow Their Tops?* New York: Scholastic, Inc., 2000.

Simon, Seymour. *Volcanoes*. New York: William Morrow & Company, 1995.

Van Rose, Susanna, and James Stevenson. *Eyewitness: Volcanoes and Earthquakes*. DK Publishing, 2000.

Wood, Lily. *Volcanoes*. New York: Scholastic Inc., 2000.

## Web Sites

**University of North Dakota. *Volcano World*.**
<http://volcano.und.nodak.edu>

***Volcanoes*.**
<http://www.learner.org/exhibits/volcanoes>

**United States Geological Survey.**
<http://volcanoes.usgs.gov>

# Index

*To my favorite young readers—Jimmy, Mick, Brendan, Joseph, and Mary Cate*

**Series Literacy Consultant:**
Allan A. De Fina, Ph.D.
Past President of the New Jersey Reading Association
Professor, Department of Literacy Education
New Jersey City University

**Science Consultant:**
Cynthia Gardner
Geologist
U.S. Geological Survey
Cascades Volcano Observatory

**Note to Teachers and Parents:** The *I Like Science!* series supports the National Science Education Standards for K–4 science, including content standards "Science as a human endeavor" and "Science as inquiry." The Words to Know section introduces subject-specific vocabulary, including pronunciation and definitions. Early readers may require help with these new words.

**Library of Congress Cataloging-in-Publication Data**

McGlone, Catherine.
    Visiting volcanoes with a scientist / Catherine McGlone.
        p. cm. — (I like science!)
    Summary: Briefly explains the work of volcano scientists, who study temperature changes, rocks, and other data to learn how volcanoes work and can warn people when a volcano may erupt.
    Includes bibliographical references and index.
    ISBN 0-7660-2269-2
    1. Volcanoes—Juvenile literature. [1. Volcanoes. 2. Volcanologists.] I. Title. II. Series.
QE521.3.M392 2004
551.21—dc21

2003011115

Printed in the United States of America

10 9 8 7 6 5 4 3 2 1

**To Our Readers:** We have done our best to make sure all Internet Addresses in this book were active and appropriate when we went to press. However, the author and the publisher have no control over and assume no liability for the material available on those Internet sites or on other Web sites they may link to. Any comments or suggestions can be sent by e-mail to comments@enslow.com or to the address on the back cover.

**Photo Credits:** © 2002–2003 ArtToday.com, Inc., p. 6; © 1999 Artville, LLC, p. 18; Enslow Publishers, Inc. pp. 21, 22; Gary Hincks/Science Photo Library, p. 8; Dr. Juerg Alean/Science Photo Library, p. 9; United States Department of the Interior, U. S. Geological Survey, David A. Johnston Cascades Volcano Observatory, Vancouver, Washington, pp.1, 2, 4, 15, 17, 19, 22, Thomas J. Casadevall, p. 12; B. Chouet, pp. 3, 13, 20–21; Austin Post, p. 7; W. E. Scott, pp. 5, 14, 16; Donald A. Swanson, pp. 10–11.

**Cover Photo:** United States Department of the Interior, U. S. Geological Survey, David A. Johnston Cascades Volcano Observatory, Vancouver, Washington.

A special thanks to David Wieprecht for his help in obtaining the illustrations.